#1 Amazon Best Selling Author

Self-Publishing: Lessons Learned From My Journey

Mary M. Gillam, Col (Ret), USAF, Ph.D.

ISBN: 1495487067
ISBN-13: 978-1495487064

For additional books by the Author, and booking, speaking, coaching or consulting information:

- Website: http://www.m2gleadershipbiz.com
- Email: DrMaryGillam@m2gleadershipbiz.com
- Email: gillammm@verizon.net
- Author's Amazon Book Page information www.amazon.com/author/marygillam
- Author's Electronic Press Kit information http://epresskitz.com/DrMaryMGillam

Books are available on Amazon, CreateSpace, Kindle, Barnes & Noble and other book distribution sites.

Book Cover: CreateSpace.com

Printed in the United States of America

Other Books by Dr. Mary M. Gillam

14 Jewels of Dynamic Leadership

Information Warfare: Combating the Threat in the 21st Century

Exploring the Impact of the Clinger-Cohen Act of 1996 on Information Technology Governance (Dissertation)

31 Gems of Poetic Inspiration

I Never Said Good-bye

A Jewel Collage of Poetry

Women Stop the Chase: Let God's Man Find You

Women Stop the Chase: Let God's Man Find You Work Book

DEDICATION

To all of the many people who have asked me to share with them how I self-published my first book.

ACKNOWLEDGMENTS

I want to simple acknowledge the many people from across the world that have inspired and encouraged me to share my self-publishing journey.

CONTENTS

DEDICATION v

ACKNOWLEDGMENTS vi

CONTENTS vii

INTRODUCTION 1

CHAPTER 1 3

Six Questions Every New Author 3

Should Ask 3

CHAPTER 2 9

Writing the First Draft of Your Manuscript 9

CHAPTER 3 13

Selecting a Self-Publishing Company 13

CHAPTER 4 21

Getting Your Book Copyrighted 21

CHAPTER 5 23

Promotion of Your Book 23

CHAPTER 6 27

Conclusions 27

APPENDIX 1 29

Six Questions Every New Author 29

Should Ask 29

APPENDIX 2 33

Some Key Websites to Remember 33
About the Author..35

INTRODUCTION

Do you like to write? If your answer is yes, then just imagine having a positive story or message locked inside of you just bursting at the seams to come out? It has been dormant for years. But with a little motivation, you have now decided to go forward and pursue your writing dreams. Unfortunately, you have come to a roadblock because you don't' know how to get started.

Self-Publishing: Lessons Learned from My Journey is designed to help you navigate the waters of getting your first book published. The book is not designed to be a complete guide to self-publishing. My goal is to simple share lessons learned that can enable you to become a published author. Having published seven previous books, I can share experiences and tools that can guide you through the self-publishing process.

If you are ready, then let's begin. I am excited to start this journey with you, and I hope that your dream to self-publish your first book is fulfilled.

Let's go!

CHAPTER 1

Six Questions Every New Author Should Ask

As a child, I loved to write. I wrote stories, poems, and even some plays. When I was in the 8th grade, I wrote a play for Thanksgiving that was presented to the entire student body. Since history was one of my favorite subjects, in high school, I wrote another play about Alexander the Great. While in college, one of my English professors wanted me to change my major to one of the literary disciplines. However, I was on a chemistry and military scholarship. Therefore, I was not about to lose that funding.

Although I loved writing, I never thought about pursuing it professionally until a few years ago. Since this was a new area for me, I began documenting much of my journey. Before, I began writing one word, I asked myself six distinct questions.

First, what story or message do I want to share? This is a very important question because it sets the stage for everything. The storyline for my first book dealt specifically with coping with grief. My grandmother, who was my legal guardian, had passed away when I was stationed in Korea. Since I never had the opportunity to say good-bye, I struggled with that sentiment for years. Writing about my experience enabled me to obtain closure and in-turn help others to deal with their grief.

Second, what problem (if any) can I solve by writing my story? What is the purpose for the book? Oftentimes, writers will hear people ask, "Why should I purchase your book? What is in it for me?" As a writer, you have to be able to adequately, effectively, and succinctly answer these questions. This will help guide you in the writing and marketing of your product.

Third, what audience do I want to reach? Every writer must identify their target market. Who is going to buy your books? Your market will drive your writing. For example, if you are targeting children, you will not write using jargon or vocabulary for adults. As with any product, you have to invest the time, effort, and resources to define your target market. You can do this yourself by conducting research on the internet or you can hire a marketing team. However, remember that there will be costs associated with every outside resource you pursue. Note this expense in your planning budget.

Fourth, why should the audience listen to me? Do you have expertise or experience in this area? These are very important questions because they lead to an author's credibility. For example, are you an expert in your field? Do you have irrefutable knowledge that can truly make a difference in someone's life or add to the body of knowledge in this area?

Fifth, what genre or category of writing do I want to specialize in? For example, do you want to be known as a non-fiction or fiction writer? Maybe you write both. What is your area (i.e. religious, leadership, women or men issues, and self-development)? It is important that you define what kind of writer you want your audience to perceive you as being. As you write, you can develop a following based on your books. Therefore, you want to make it easy for readers to find your products.

Finally, the last question that I recommend every new author ask is, "Am I writing for profit or pleasure?" This is a very important question because it will drive your activity. If you are writing for profit, then you are going to basically engaged in your writing activities as if you are operating a business. Since this is not a book on business, I am not going to expound more on this topic. On the other hand, if you are writing for pleasure, then you may not necessarily be as concerned about a lot of the things that would drive someone who is writing for profit. Although you would like to earn money for your work, you may have a different perspective on the return on your investment. In other words, you may not be willing to spend as much on marketing as someone who is actually writing for a living. Regardless of the category you fall in, it is important to establish a budget.

The above six questions are not all inconclusive. They simple represent a dialogue that I engaged in as I was deliberating publishing my first book. By taking time to go through this process, you will have a good frame of reference for which to analyze your decision to self-publish. For your convenience, the questions have been summarized in Appendix 1.

CHAPTER 2

Writing the First Draft of Your Manuscript

Before you began writing one word, it is important that you find a place to write. I prefer to write in a location away from distractions. This allows me to build my product by focusing on the storyline, its characters, and the message I want to convey to my reading audience.

Writing the first draft of your manuscript can be daunting. There will be times, when you will want to throw in the towel. My advice is to continue writing. The words will come and you will begin to see your book come to life.

There are many word processing packages on the market today. Since I am familiar with Word, I simply use it to develop my draft manuscripts. If you are not familiar with a word processing package, I recommend that you get training in this area. It will be difficult to produce a book without having a degree of familiarity with a word processing package.

How are your writing skills? Depending on your abilities, you may want to get an editor to review your manuscript before you go final. When you self-publish your book, you assume a lot of responsibility unless you are willing to purchase additional resources. For example, most publishers recommend that you get family, friends, and an editor to review your work.

As the author of a book, sometimes, we are too close to the work to be objective and critical. Yet, in order to produce the best product possible, you want to have some external "eyes" review your manuscript for clarity, logical flow, punctuation, storyline, etc. This step can save you a lot of time and possible embarrassment especially if the manuscript is full of errors or it does not flow correctly.

When having someone review your manuscript, it is important to maintain an open mind. Some people refer to this as having a "thick skin." Keep in mind, that when you publish a work, it represents you and your credibility with your audience. If the manuscript is replete or full of errors, it may cause readers to question your professionalism and commitment to produce a credible book.

Remember, it may take several drafts before you finalize your manuscript. The time you invest in making the product your very best will produce great rewards. You will be proud to cite this work as your own.

CHAPTER 3

Selecting a Self-Publishing Company

When I decided to self-publish, I began inquiring about different companies. I reviewed several books produced by different publishers. After completing my research, I decided to investigate the capabilities of CreateSpace which is an Amazon affiliate and a print on demand publisher. The website for CreateSpace is www.createspace.com.

CreateSpace is a self-publishing site that makes it fairly easy for authors to produce their books. Since I had gone through the traditional publishing methodology prior, I was familiar with the requirements for book publication. What attracted me to CreateSpace was not only the product that they produced, but the publishing tools that they make available for authors. An author can either go through the publishing process independently or you can purchase additional help along the way.

As with Amazon, you need to first create a member account on the CreateSpace website. You will also need to create a password. Afterwards, you can begin the process of reviewing the steps to getting your book published. The site is easy to navigate, and there are instructions to walk you through the process.

In general, you will enter the title of the book, subtitle, and other pertinent information that pertains to your registering your new book in CreateSpace. A nice feature of CreateSpace is that the company will provide you with a free International Standard Book Number (ISBN) which enables other publishers to find your book. However, if you want to purchase your own ISBN, you can go through a company called Bowker, which is located at www.myidentifiers.com. In the past, I have actually done both especially when producing electronic books.

After completing this step, you need to decide on the size of your book. Six by nine is considered a standard size. However, there are many other options to choose from.

Once you decide on your book size, you can now upload the manuscript for review. This is referred to as the "interior" of the book. The online reviewer will search for formatting, alignment, grammatical errors, etc. If you have inserted pictures into your manuscript, the reviewer will provide comments on the quality of the pictures. If the original picture is of poor quality, then it will be reflected in the book. As with any online reviewer tool, you are given the opportunity to approve the document or revise the work. You can do this step as many times as required. While the manuscript is being reviewed, you can now begin work on your book cover.

CreateSpace has a book cover tool called Cover Creator. With this tool, you can use either the sample templates from CreateSpace or you can upload your own book cover. I have used both formats in my books. When doing the book cover in CreateSpace, you have to also provide details about the book. On every book, you traditionally see a small amount of verbiage detailing the book's content very succinctly. You may also need to provide information about the author. This is dependent upon which format you choose to use for your book cover.

Regarding book covers, I have also used a service have Fiverr, which is located at http://fiverr.com/. This is a graphics, marketing, and designing site that offers a myriad of services to include book covers. For the majority of the products that I have received, I have been very pleased. Additionally, the fees are very reasonable (i.e. as low as $5).

Once you are satisfied with your manuscript and book cover, CreateSpace will ask if you are ready to approve the final proof of your product. You can do this either electronically or order a book proof for $2.15. I normally order the book proof so that I can see exactly what the book will look like. The first time I did this proved invaluable because some of the text was too low on one of the pages. If I had not ordered the proof, I would not have been able to adequately see the error. Therefore, I strongly recommend that you order a proof of your book. As a side note, when I do book signings, I traditionally allow customers to review the proof. Therefore, I eliminate the problem of potentially having my actual products damaged in the review process (especially if the customer decides not to purchase).

While you are waiting to receive your proof, there are a few other steps that you can complete with your CreateSpace account. If you have not done this previously, you need to identify where CreateSpace needs to send your royalties. You will have to have an account capable of receiving the payments (i.e. merchant account).

Additionally, you can start work on the final setup of your book to include, distribution, pricing, and description. This section is self-explanatory. Therefore, you should not have any difficulties navigating the information. As the author of your book, you are in the best position to provide the critical details that are required to complete the description phase of the book. This is the information that is available to readers. It also includes the author's biography.

During this phase, you will also have to decide what category in which to place your book. Spend some time in this section. You need to select the appropriate category. If your book is in the wrong category, more than likely it will be difficult for readers to find your book. CreateSpace also allows you to develop tag words so that readers can search for your book. When selecting tag words, place yourself in the shoes of your reader. For example, if they typed in specific words regarding your book, would they find it?

At this point, I think I have addressed many of the steps that I used to publish my book with CreateSpace. For your convenience, I summarized the websites identified in this chapter in Appendix 2. If I omitted a step in the CreateSpace self-publishing process, I apologize. However, since the site is not complicated to use, you should not have a problem getting your manuscript through the portals of CreateSpace.

In summary, let me reiterate that because of my familiarity with CreateSpace that is the reason why I chose to describe my work with their company. I have been very pleased with their services. However, there are many self-publishing companies. Therefore, I recommend that you invest the time in finding the one that you are comfortable with.

CHAPTER 4

Getting Your Book Copyrighted

How many of you know someone who may have had their book idea stolen? Although this is a negative thing to happen, I can assure you it does happen. In many instance, the individual never bothered to get their book idea copyrighted.

This process is straightforward. You begin by going to the copyright.gov website which is located at http://www.copyright.gov/. After creating an account to include a password, you are able to begin the registration process.

You have the option of filing your manuscript either via mail or electronically.

eCO Login

Electronic Copyright Office

Since I have filed my manuscripts or literary works both ways, I tend to now file my forms electronically. It expedites the process. Additionally, the fee is normally no more than $35.00.

Another point that I need to make is that you can register or copyright a work as either a draft or in its final composition. I have done both. You will be required to upload a copy of the document. One lesson that I learned from this process is that the copyright office database only accepts documents uploading from Internet Explorer. For example, when I tried to upload my documents from Bing, it never worked. After inquiring with the copyright office technical support team, they informed me that their system only accepted documents from Internet Explorer. Therefore, I had to use Internet Explorer to log in to my copyright.gov account so that I could upload the manuscript. This technical limitation may have recently changed. However, this was my experience.

CHAPTER 5

Promotion of Your Book

Now that you have published your first book, what is the next step? Typically you would have begun promoting your book prior to its release. The time frame can vary. However, if you are an unknown author, I am not sure it really matters unless you already have an established platform.

As you can imagine, marketing is expensive. When writing a book, you have to decide on what your budget is going to be. You can easily invest thousands of dollars in the production, packaging, and marketing of your book. Sometimes the return on investment (ROI) is great. At other times, the ROI may be very minimal. Therefore, it is crucial that you decide the status of your budget.

Personally, I have invested in both paid advertising and free promotions. For example, I initially submitted press releases (announcing my book) through the free press release services. I later contacted two paid press release services that tailored to my particular audience.

Living in the era of social media, I immediately began taking advantage of these platforms. Although I had a Facebook account, I was not very active until I released my book. I found that it was a great tool to use to advertise the book. I later established a Twitter account and began an aggressive campaign promoting the book. Additionally, I used my LinkedIn and Google+ accounts to promote as well.

On many of the social networking sites, you can advertise for free just via posting content. However, if you want to get more strategic and focused in your promotion efforts, you can buy these services through the various sites. Having a promotion and marketing strategy prior to release of your book is extremely important. It will help you to not only strategize your efforts, but to keep a firm eye on your budget.

If your book is of keen interest to a large audience, there is the possibility that media may come to you. I conducted several free radio interviews based on my #1 Amazon best-selling book, *Women Stop the Chase: Let God's Man Find You*. On several instances, I was told that the title was very intriguing which in-turn drove the request for numerous interviews.

Let me make one more comment about Fiverr. I mentioned this site earlier. There are a variety of people advertising their services on Fiverr to include radio talk show hosts. This is definitely a source of promotion especially if you have a small budget. As a new author, the goal is to get as much publicity as you can for a budget that you can live with.

I have seen many people over extend themselves in trying to promote their book. I firmly believe that you should be responsible for your finances and be selective about how you want to invest those dollars. However, if you have the resources to invest in a well-organized promotion and marketing campaign plan, then I encourage you to pursue that avenue, but do it wisely.

CHAPTER 6

Conclusions

Congratulations! You are now equipped with a basic understanding of what is required to self-publish your book. As I indicated earlier, the purpose of my book was to simple share with you some lessons that I learned on my self-publishing journey. This book was not designed to be all inconclusive, but to provide you with a working knowledge of how to get the process started.

Although I have used other publishing sites, in this book, I chose to highlight those in which I have had extensive experience. Since I was very familiar with CreateSpace, Fiverr, and several of the social media networking platforms, I focused specifically on their capabilities. However, there are many other self-publishing sites that you can use to complete your publishing journey.

Additionally, I recommend that if you are a serious writer, continue to invest in resources that will help you grow as a writer and self-publisher. This is extremely important. Always remember that credibility is everything.

As one author to another, I wish you all the success in the world as you self-publish your first book. You will never forget that moment. This accomplishment will leave a monumental impression on you documenting your ability to inspire others through the written word.

APPENDIX 1

Six Questions Every New Author Should Ask

1. What story or message do I want to share?

2. What problem (if any) can I solve by writing my story?

3. What audience do I want to reach?

4. Why should the audience listen to me?

5. What genre or category of writing do I want to specialize in?

6. Am I writing for profit or pleasure?

APPENDIX 2

Some Key Websites to Remember

1. www.createSpace.com

2. www.fiverr.com

3. www.copyrightgov.com

4. www.myidentifiers.com

About the Author

Dr. Mary M. Gillam is a former Senior Executive Service (SES) member with the Department of Defense. She is also a retired Air Force Colonel. She is the president and CEO of M2G Dynamic Leadership Solutions, which is a veteran owned small business consulting firm specializing in information technology, management, and leadership development located outside the Washington, DC metropolitan area. Dr. Gillam is also a Certified John C. Maxwell Leadership Coach, Trainer, and Speaker. An avid writer, she is the author of seven books.

Made in the USA
Middletown, DE
16 March 2016